SCIENCE FROM GOD'S PERSPECTIVE

SCIENCE FROM GOD'S PERSPECTIVE

LUKE JOHNSON

This book is dedicated to the full use of my Lord and Savior,
Jesus Christ: the Living God.

CONTENTS

Author to the Reader

This book is a work of theological philosophy (epistemology and apologetics), in which my desire is to encourage people to think more deeply about the God they serve. There is no shortage of controversy within the body of Christ. In this work, there will likely be areas some may find unacceptable. However, I stand by the words I have written, because I believe, with every fiber of my soul, that the concepts discussed herein are true.

As the reader will discover, I am a firm, foundational Christian. I do not claim to belong to any denomination. I only claim to follow the Lord Jesus Christ. I believe the Holy Bible is the inspired Word of God and needs to be given the proper respect that entails. I try my utmost to take God and His Word seriously. I speak these things in hope that the reader too, will take God seriously and will be able to expand their mind to better understand the nature of God.

This book is written to explore areas of theology and science, in an attempt to answer questions which have plagued humanity for some time. I hope the reader will look, contemplate, and search for themselves the main focal point into which this work delves: the mind of the Living God. For it seems to me, that in this time of world history, there is a lack of understanding of the God Christians profess to serve.

While primarily centered towards a more seasoned Christian audience, I believe nearly anyone attempting to understand God better can learn from these writings. The topics contained within cover more in depth thoughts and reasonings than one may expect from a book of this size. Common topics, such as marriage and daily living are not addressed herein. Moreover, there are only seven chapters to this book. Each chapter delves into a new set of weighty, thought provoking subjects; and as such, the reader is encouraged to reread and study them closely.

While I do not claim to be any type of theologian, or seminary professor, or possess such official degrees or training, I have been raised by a Christian family who instilled within me the truth of God and His Word. Yet, each individual must make their own decision to follow God, being responsible only for what that individual thinks, says, or does. Despite what may be desired, one cannot force anyone else to follow the Lord. I believe that all ought to look more closely at themselves (on the inside) rather than continuously looking at others (on the outside). In this way, we may better learn what it means to be a Christian, not from seeing, but from doing.

There are several axioms (or "cornerstones") with which this philosophical building must be constructed. The main cornerstone is humility. Without it, the observer (and writer) will miss many important clues. One must be willing to admit a lack of understanding about something and work around the obstacle. A second main cornerstone is the Holy Bible. I believe the Bible is the holy, inspired (God breathed) Word of God. It needs to be treated with respect and as the ultimate authority on matters. This should be an unwavering commitment. I do not deem it wise to take a critical view of Holy Writ without due cause.

I believe it is important to begin with the concept of the Bible as Truth, because the Bible _claims_ to be true. Applying the cornerstone of humility here: I must admit that I don't want to argue too much with God if I can help it; especially considering I'm not as versed on the subject as He is. Alongside this notion, I also happen to love the Constitution of the United States, which dictates innocence until proven guilty. Granting a benefit of the doubt, until proven otherwise, I see no reason to deny this right to the Bible. The Bible is the only tried and true book that claims to be the holy, inspired Word of God. It is still believed to be such by a great deal of people today. It has stood this test of time for thousands of years. No other text has that pedigree or track record.

The Scriptures themselves say to test them. "Beloved, believe not every spirit, but try the spirits whether they are of God" (I John 4:1) and "In the mouth of two or three witnesses shall every word be established" (II Corinthians 13:1b). In following the advice provided by the text itself, what are God's witnesses? Humanity has what God has made, and what God wrote about: the creation, the industrial end product; and the Bible, the manual to said product. With an open mind, looking at these two things, what can be found?

The Bible provides a unique view into God's perspective on things. By using the Scriptures as a firm base, we can see what God says about Himself. There are a great many things which mankind has said about God, but I think it is always important to see an individual's own point of view. God has given us the unique opportunity to see His point of view through the Holy Scriptures.

As this work is meant to encourage thought, it is also meant to encourage discussion and further research. Due to the nature of the subject, it is inexhaustible in depth. As such, there was no attempt made to touch every corner of the topics within; because, doing so would take away from the main focal points of each chapter. This book must needs be read with an open mind, and if one can, as the Bereans did, search the Scriptures to see if the things spoken are true. I challenge each individual reader to discover for him or herself the truth of the Scriptures referenced within these pages. The Authorized King James Version of the Bible is used for all Scriptural references contained herein.

CHAPTER 1

Who is This God I Serve?

There is no easy way to describe who God is. He is beyond a simple description. Although many people would agree with this statement, it does not stop them from attempting to put God in a box. It is my firm belief that because of this, great masses of people have little to no understanding of the God they serve. I want to start with showing different characteristics of God. This list will be extensive, but by no means exhaustive, because God is inexhaustible. This is merely to provoke the reader into further study and contemplation.

Beginning, God is a *legal* God. This is evidenced with the book of Leviticus and in the foundational laws which govern creation. The laws of God show that He is completely *just* and therefore must be *honest* as well. From these characteristics, it is plain that God is a deeply *logical* God. He even went so far as to invent logical reasoning, coupled with the ability to formulate ideas and hold memories for future access. This logic however, does not inhibit His creativity.

God is a *creative* God, Who designed everything, and that cannot be done without inexhaustible ingenuity. The very notion of creativity itself is something God created, much like logical reasoning. These things together, indicate that God is *philosophical*. In fact, the philosophy of God is visible in the books of Proverbs and Ecclesiastes. To do all this, He indeed must be the very wise, *All-Knowing* God.

God is a poetic God as shown in Psalm 19:1, "The heavens declare the glory of God, the firmament sheweth His handiwork." What is this if not a physical manifestation of God's poetry? The universe itself is a poetic canvas painted with the colors of the stars.

The All-Knowing God is also the *All*-powerful God. He must be to have created all that is. His power is incalculable and defies comparison. People may think the devil is somehow equivalent to God, but this is pure folly. A power struggle between the devil and God is a no-contest. God wins. Period. There is nothing the devil can do in a one-on-one with God. Furthermore, there is nothing stopping God's power, except His own restraint. As God is powerful, it goes without saying that God is strong and mighty. More so, God is a warrior, "The LORD is a man of war: the LORD is his name" (Exodus 15:3). Yet, God is also peaceable (Romans 16:20).

God is merciful (Hosea 6:6) and forgiving (I John 1:9). These are in complete compatibility with God's justice, seen best in I John 1:9. In addition to these characteristics, God is a jealous God (Exodus 20:5). He is jealous for the protection of His people, the saints: Jews and Christians alike, as well as humanity as a whole (Psalm 140). God is a God of covenant, shown by the Bible itself being split between the Old Covenant (Testament) and the New Covenant (Testament). God's jealousy is coupled with God's love. The most widely known, and commonly misunderstood, aspect of God is His love (visible in John 3:16). It seems pertinent to point out that love doesn't mean He always does things we like. Rather, He does things He knows are best for us. This may be difficult to understand at times, but it is how our humility and trust grow toward maturity.

Moreover, God is a *joyous* God (Nehemiah 8:10) and a *fun* God. Looking at creation and life in general, it becomes clear that God likes to have fun and wants us to do likewise. Subsequently, God is *adventurous* and has a deep sense of *humor* and *irony*, as evident from the many stories in Scripture. In these adventures too, is evidence of a *thorough* God that plans ahead, a *helpful* God, and a *protective* God (Psalm 46:1).

God is a righteous God (Jeremiah 23:6). He is a generous God (Psalm 84:11). God is a healing God (Exodus 15:26, Luke 4:18). He is also uncompromising and unchanging and keeps His Word. He has a full expectation that we should strive to be like Him, if we have His nature within us (Revelation 3:10), despite Him being a holy God. Since mankind was made in His image, He commands us to be holy, as He is holy (Leviticus 11:44, I Peter 1:16). This is only possible because God is not far from us: He is *Emmanuel*, God with[in] us. He is a very personal God (Acts 17:27), who dwells within the hearts of His people. His presence is felt everywhere and in everything (John 1:1-5). He is the All-Knowing, All-Powerful, *Ever-Present*, God.

Each of the foregoing statements is very powerful and can be life changing, if allowed. Beyond these aspects of God's nature are things which God *is not*, and without full understanding it can be tempting to place God within the confines of a human lens. God is not a god who lies (Number 23:19). God is not clueless (Matthew 10:29), nor is He foolish: God's wisdom far surpasses our own (Isaiah 55:8-9). God also is not prideful, nor is He vain or petty (Proverbs 6:16-19). God is not distracted or aloof (I Kings 18:27-39), nor is He "a God that hath pleasure in wickedness: neither shall evil dwell with [Him]" (Psalm 5:4). These aspects help define who God is not and are important to remember.

Who God is and who God isn't, is drawn along a line which is eerily similar to things which commonly befall mankind. Humanity's own shortcomings are brought sharper into focus, highlighting God's love for us that much more. God's love for mankind is so strong that He does not want to leave us in our state of despair. In love, He reached down in an effort to pull us up to Him, by the sacrifice He made in coming as the God-man Jesus Christ: being crucified and rising from the dead. The truth of this, brings to mind many parables of Jesus which establish a need to change our lives, in response to God's intervention. The Christian life in not one of our own works, but rather of God, working in us, to clean us up and enable us to live free from the bondage of sin.

When the whole Bible is taken as what it claims to be (the Holy inspired Word of God), then one must wrestle with the issues surrounding justice, judgment, righteousness, mercy, etc. The aspects of God spoken of previously make this reconciliation of natures difficult. However, the Jesus of the New Testament is the same God as in the Old Testament. John 1:1-5 makes this point clear:

"1 In the beginning was the Word, and the Word was with God, and the Word was God. 2 The same was in the beginning with God. 3 All things were made by him; and without him was not any thing made that was made. 4 In him was life; and the life was the light of men. 5 And the light shineth in darkness; and the darkness comprehended it not."

God the Father and Jesus are one, a point made clear in many other Scriptures. It forces one to acknowledge that Jesus, with His sermons on love, forgiveness, mercy, oneness among the brethren, and all the rest, is in the same context of God from the Old Testament. He is the same God who ordered Joshua to lead Israel as a sword of judgment against everyone in the land of Canaan (Deuteronomy 20:16-18). As an aside on this particular point of God's justice: the LORD told Abraham in Genesis 15:13-16:

"13... Know of a surety that thy seed shall be a stranger in a land that is not theirs, and shall serve them; and they shall afflict them four hundred years; 14 And also that nation, whom they shall serve, will I judge: and afterward shall they come out with great substance. 15 And thou shalt go to thy fathers in peace; thou shalt be buried in a good old age. 16 But in the fourth generation they shall come hither again: for the iniquity of the Amorites is not yet full."

Therefore, it becomes apparent from God's perspective that the Amorites had over four hundred years to repent before God told Israel to wipe them out. The exact crimes of the Amorites (later called Canaanites) is not fully known to the modern reader. However, from a judicial perspective, God as a righteous judge deemed that the *behaviors*, not the individuals, required capitol punishment. While carried out on a national level, the justice of God appears to focus more on the collective community as a whole; with individuals as partakers from a larger volume of evil. Another good example of this type of justice is seen in the destruction of Sodom in Genesis 18 and 19. In fact, in Deuteronomy 9:4-5, this point is even more clear as Moses speaks to Israel:

"4 Speak not thou in thine heart, after that the LORD thy God hath cast them out from before thee, saying, For my righteousness the LORD hath brought me in to possess this land: but for the wickedness of these nations the LORD doth drive them out from before thee. 5 Not for thy righteousness, or for the uprightness of thine heart, dost thou go to possess their land: but for the wickedness of these nations the LORD thy God doth drive them out from before thee, and that he may perform the word which the LORD sware unto thy fathers, Abraham, Isaac, and Jacob."

We see here that God is just, both objectively (in judging the wicked for their deeds), and also subjectively. Subjective justice is visible through God keeping His covenant with Abraham, by giving the promised land to the Israelites. Both types of justice are present in God's reasoning. It is also plainly seen that God doesn't allow people to wipe nations from the face of the earth just because they think they are somehow better than another. This very important concept is sometimes misconstrued. God doesn't say genocide is good: He told Israel to judge the Canaanites, because they were wicked. Their behaviors dictated His judicial response. God doesn't hold different groups to different standards (Romans 2:11). The role gets reversed with Nebuchadnezzar in Jeremiah 25 (Nebuchadrezzar and Nebuchadnezzar are the same person):

"8 Therefore thus saith the LORD of hosts; Because ye have not heard my words, 9 Behold, I will send and take all the families of the north, saith the LORD, and Nebuchadrezzar the king of Babylon, my servant, and will bring them against this land, and against the inhabitants thereof, and against all these nations round about, and will utterly destroy them, and make them an astonishment, and an hissing, and perpetual desolations. 10 Moreover I will take from them the voice of mirth, and the voice of gladness, the voice of the bridegroom, and the voice of the bride, the sound of the millstones, and the light of the candle. 11 And this whole land shall be a desolation, and an astonishment; and these nations shall serve the king of Babylon seventy years."

Just as Israel was called upon to judge Canaan, so God called on Babylon to judge Israel (Kingdom of Judah) for doing the same wickedness. In context, there is a need to understand another concept paramount to discerning who God is and how He deals with His creation: God's sovereignty. What does it mean to say, God is sovereign? In a nutshell, it can be understood very simply, but with great ramifications. If one accepts that God created the universe, things living and non-living, then one must accept that God, as the outright owner of everything, has authority over all things. In short then, despite whatever laws humanity creates, or even those laws God creates for humanity, He Himself is not bound by those laws, unless He so chooses. An example of this is the numerable covenants God forged with people throughout the Scriptures. Covenants, or contracts, bind both individuals to a set of regulations, in reference to one another. Without the contract, there is no legal binding.

Beyond these covenants, God is not required to do anything outside His own will. God does righteous things, because He *is* righteous. God created laws and justice, because He *is* just and legal. There is no law binding Him, or any kind of abstract responsibility tying Him, to perform a certain way. In contrast, mankind is bound by an infinite number of laws beyond its control. Physical laws governing the universe come to mind. Apart from this, as referenced earlier, God has created moral codes and has expectations for mankind to follow them. These laws, at least in God's eyes, are binding to a degree for mankind, but are not binding for God.

Does this mean that God is free to disregard His own laws? In point of fact, yes. Because God wrote the book, He can rewrite the book, and use the book, however He sees fit. He is the King and sovereign. While confounding to the modern ideals of legalism and justice in many ways, it does not make God inherently unjust or unrighteous. Since God is the author from the beginning, He is beyond a temporal moral code, thus God's *requirement* to adhere to modern ideals is irrelevant. This, in point of fact, highlights more starkly God's behavior in these spheres. The book of Job lightly confronts the issue, as God *allowed* the devil to harm Job in many ways. God however, did not do it out of pleasure, or laziness, or some other such negative human initiative, but instead God did it for Job's long term (eternal) benefit. If one can look beyond the creation that currently exists, to instead look at the creation which *will* exist (as God does), then that will help illuminate God's perspective.

If there is another world after the one currently inhabited, then this one is temporary. Each and every one of our lives is temporary. If God, willing to secure for us more *permanent* holdings, causes our temporary ones to be threatened, or even destroyed, has He done wrong? Has He not rather worked for our benefit? Our view may be of an injustice, but that does not mean that a true injustice was done. If the emotions of individuals dictated right and wrong, there would be no need of judicial systems to sort it all out.

In continuing this concept, God is no respecter of persons; He has rules and will make sure they are followed. Yet, within this view of God as the sovereign judge, II Peter 3:9 states, "9 The Lord... is longsuffering to us-ward, <u>not willing that any should perish, but that all should come to repentance</u>." It is clear therefore, that God wishes for all to repent and be saved by the door He created, that is the Lord Jesus Christ (John 10:7-9). Because Jesus *is* God in the flesh, God in bodily form. Jesus is all that God is, in a physical body (John 1).

Jesus came here and taught, was ridiculed and mocked, betrayed by a friend, beaten, scourged, and murdered, by the very people He was sent to save. How unfathomable is the unconditional love of God! Referencing back to Israel and their judgment at the hands of Babylon, God prophesied that Israel would turn away from Him, even as Moses stood judging the nation in the desert. It ought to be noted, that because Israel was under a covenant (contract) with God, their eventual idolatry and wickedness was a breach of said covenant or contract. Deuteronomy 31:16-19 explains:

"16 And the LORD said unto Moses, Behold, thou shalt sleep with thy fathers; and this people will rise up, and go a whoring after the gods of the strangers of the land, whither they go to be among them, and will forsake me, and break my covenant which I have made with them. 17 Then my anger shall be kindled against them in that day, and I will forsake them, and I will hide my face from them, and they shall be devoured, and many evils and troubles shall befall them; so that they will say in that day, Are not these evils come upon us, because our God is not among us? 18 And I will surely hide my face in that day for all the evils which they shall have wrought, in that they are turned unto other gods."

Deuteronomy 32 continues with a song God gives Moses to recite, outlining Israel's history. In this prophetic song, it states the Gospel would be given to the Gentiles, because Israel would reject the Messiah. This message is proclaimed many other times by the Old Testament prophets. When God spoke to Moses at the burning bush, it is clear that the crucifixion of Jesus was on God's mind. The name "I AM that I AM" is made up of the Hebrew letters *Yod, Hay, Vav, Hay*. This is the name YHWH, from which Jehovah is derived. Jehovah means, "the Almighty God" and "the Self-Existent One" or even (borrowing from the late Leslie Hale) "the One who has the final word." This is the name God gives to Moses in Exodus 3:14.

Ancient Hebrew letters were originally pictures and would convey additional ideas, beyond the overall definition of a word. The name "I AM that I AM" can be expressed in Hebrew to mean, "Behold the nails in my hands reveal [who I AM]." In ancient cultures, names often included implied meanings, which were taken as referring to the individual possessing the name. Likewise, the names of individuals could be connected to a specific deity, which would be unnamed, but implied as well. These customs are present when God reveals His name to Moses, and by choosing to use this particular name, the LORD shows His mindset, looking forward in time.

Keep in mind, God had not yet revealed Himself to the Israelites when He is speaking to Moses. Thus, the name I AM shouldn't be completely understood as a pretext of prior actions, but also taken as a foretelling of future ones. Not unlike when a parent names their child, despite the child not yet having done anything, the name can have significance for their future. The mind of God was evident when the resurrected Jesus allayed Thomas' doubts by showing him the scars of His crucifixion, and Thomas responded with awe, "My Lord and my God" (John 20:27-28). The Passover, the Red Sea crossing, the wilderness wandering, all of it, was a revelation of God to Israel in a way unseen before or since. Yet, the same people God had rescued from slavery and revealed Himself to, in a way unparalleled in world history, would cry loudly, "Crucify Him!" This call was for the very blood of God to be shed. In so doing, Israel would lay the blood of God on themselves and their generations after them (Matthew 27:25). Jesus' statement in John 15:13 becomes far more potent when He says, "greater love hath no man than this, that a man lay down his life for his friends."

Israel was called God's firstborn at the burning bush in Exodus 4. All that God would do for Israel (and all Israel would do to Him) was on His mind at the burning bush: from the great redemption of Israel to their great betrayal at the end. Ezekiel 16 is a sobering lamentation God writes about Israel that brings some fresh perspective to the love of God. Along with the book of Hosea, both are too lengthy to dissect here, but each adds a new dimension to the many parables of Jesus Christ. How does one connect the Old Testament wrath of God with Jesus and His love of humanity? We see that God loved Israel in the Exodus and afterwards, yet still sent them into Assyria and Babylon, eventually scattering them across the globe. As foretold in Deuteronomy, God gave full disclosure of Israel's turbulent existence. One should also keep in mind what else the Bible says about God: Jesus describes Him as our Heavenly Father (Matthew 11), a Father who is very involved and not distant from His creation: a pattern consistent throughout Scripture. In fact, through reading the Psalms there is a clear sense that God's only distance from us is imposed by us, not Him. Our relationship becomes strained, not by Him being far and away, but rather humanity being as children who run away. Scripture is clear, with Psalm 51 as a good example.

In reconciling God's direct actions, it makes more sense in the context of God as a good Father. It would explain his different behaviors and thoughts toward mankind. If we are unruly children (as God says Israel was) then the pouring out of God's wrath is not born of a random mood swing. Rather, despite God repeatedly sending people to warn us and creating a manual, we, full of pride and foolishness, ignore the warnings and continue headlong. God, our loving Father, is trying to teach us how to live beyond our sins and physical existence. As such, when the issue of prolonged disobedience comes up, we eventually get a spanking. We need to be reminded that God is serious, because we seldom take Him seriously until something drastic happens. It doesn't have to happen this way, but when a child openly defies a parent, there is discipline of some kind. The discipline must be something that hurts and makes the parent's point clear. God is serious. The life we have in this world is temporary and God will mess it up in order to teach us something. One look at Noah's flood will showcase that nicely (Genesis 6-9).

Learning lessons from ancient Israel, if God was taken more seriously, He wouldn't have to reveal Himself in ways that are painful. Instead, He would reveal Himself to us in the way He prefers: tenderly. God is no respecter of persons: Christian, Jew, Muslim, Hindu, Buddhist, atheist, etc., all have to answer for their works someday, no matter what. It's just that true Christians have acknowledged God's loving side and accepted His free gift of reconciliation, that could only be done by Himself, as Jesus the Christ. Reconciliation with God is not a free pass to live the way one wishes. It's a mark that says a person belongs to God and is working on getting their life turned around, with God's help. God doesn't expect us to be clean when we come to Him, but He expects our cooperation with Him as He cleans us up. This ongoing process of sanctification is evidence of God's love and grace.

CHAPTER 2

What Does the Universe Show Us About God?

What can be seen in nature that tells us about God? Beginning with the universe, what is the universe? Is there more than one? What dictates what is within (or without) the universe? The term *universe* is a compound word of Latin root origin, meaning: a single (uni) spoken sentence (verse). The word *universe* literally means, "a single spoken sentence." Without complicating this text with differing conjectures, the definition of the universe appears to be all that God spoke into being. So, laying aside parallel universes and the like, these would all be contained within the meaning of the (singular) universe, because they would be within every thing God created.

Building on this concept, does one construct the universe by what is seen tangibly (the five senses only)? Or is the universe defined by what actually is (including heaven and hell, etc.)? The term *universe* is not present in the Scriptures anywhere. Instead, the term cosmos is used in the New Testament to describe God's creation. John 3:16, with which most are familiar states, "For God so loved the World that He gave His only begotten Son, that whosoever believeth in Him should not perish, but have everlasting life."

The term *world* in the above passage, relates to the Greek word *cosmos*, meaning the universe. However, more than the universe as a location or space, *cosmos* includes all the laws and order found within the universe as well. More accurately, *cosmos* refers to a perspective of the universe as a thing and as a state of being. The Greek understanding of the universe at the time is that it always existed and always will; therefore the universe is self-existing. This Greek view of the universe was disproven by a 1948 discovery of the cosmic background microwave radiation (called CMB). Microwave radiation, visible throughout outer space, was shown to have come from a singular origin. The existence of this singular radiating source is evidence of a beginning to the universe (Wollack, 2016). The background radiation was observed by the Hubble space telescope in 1965, proving beyond any reasonable doubt that the universe had a specific time of origin. It is because of this discovery that astrophysicists conjectured what has become known as "the Big Bang" theory.

Despite the hypotheses of mankind, a beginning to the universe is described clearly in Genesis 1:1, "In the beginning God created the heaven and the earth." The discovery of the CMB was scientific proof of the universe's creation, compatible with the Biblical text. What's more, is how creation plays out in the Scriptures. Notice the term "heaven" is used in the singular in Genesis 1:1, because "heavens" does not come about until after the creation of the firmaments on day 2. "6 And God said, Let there be a firmament in the midst of the waters, and let it divide the waters from the waters. 7 And God made the firmament, and divided the waters which were under the firmament from the waters which were above the firmament: and it was so. 8 And God called the firmament Heaven. And the evening and the morning were the second day" (Genesis 1:6-8). Therefore, an understanding of heaven can be simplified into, essentially, an "empty space." This would include outer space, Earth's atmosphere, and the third heaven where God sits on His throne (II Corinthians 12:2).

It is important in the definition of the universe that "Heaven" is included in God's creation, because God did not originally reside in heaven when He made the universe. The third heaven is part of the universe. It is directly connected to outer space, and subsequently the earth in a real, tangible, albeit hidden, sense. While there are more dimensions to the universe with which we are unable to interact, these dimensions do exist on Earth, in space, and would therefore also exist in "Heaven." The idea of our universe having more dimensions than we currently, consciously, experience is not new. Harvard physicist Lisa Randall describes this concept in an interview by the Smithsonian, "'There could be more to the universe than the three dimensions we are familiar with. They are hidden from us in some way, perhaps because they're tiny or warped. But even if they're invisible, they could affect what we actually observe in the universe. There are lots of things we cannot see with the naked eye that turn out to be based in reality'" (Irion, 2011). The question of how the third heaven fits into the universe can be further evaluated when considering the scientific quandaries of dimensions beyond the obvious.

It would seem inopportunistic to not point out the fact that anything described in the Bible as God, or angels, or devils, would be inter-dimensional beings. There are some who argue that aliens, or futuristic humans, or so forth are the creators of the universe, along with whatever other strange theories are adrift. In a simple line of logic however, God is a multi-dimensional being. He is far beyond anything we can see on Earth or in outer space. He is the Creator (and thus outside) of time, space, and matter. Thus He is all-present (omnipresent), all-knowing (omniscient), and all-powerful (omnipotent). Taking the Bible at face value, God's multi-dimensional make-up and influence on the universe is a simple step in logic. Ongoing scientific studies into how dimensions interact back-up this view of the Biblical frame-work. The same cannot be said of angels and devils, who are bound by the laws of the universe, because they were created within it by God, who is (naturally) outside it.

How this relates to the third heaven and the universe as a whole is seen in Psalm 113:6 in a description of God, "6 Who humbleth himself to behold the things that are in heaven, and in the earth!" If God humbles Himself to behold the things that are in heaven, then He must be based in something outside the third heaven. The implications of this concept are rarely considered. Every law governing the universe does not govern God. God wrote the laws. He decided what they should be, but He never bound himself to those laws, except when He came as the man Jesus Christ.

Isaiah the prophet has another excellent description of God, "15 For thus saith the high and lofty One that inhabiteth eternity, whose name is Holy; I dwell in the high and holy place, with him also that is of a contrite and humble spirit, to revive the spirit of the humble, and to revive the heart of the contrite ones" (Isaiah 57:15). Drawing attention to the first part of the above verse: God inhabits eternity. That is an interesting way to describe Him. Revelation 21:1 states, "1 And I saw a new heaven and a new earth: for the first heaven and the first earth were passed away; and there was no more sea." The third heaven, which now exists, will not exist anymore. Therefore, in order for God to create a new universe, without ceasing to exist Himself, He must have an original habitation outside the third heaven, and thus outside the entire universe. That habitation is eternity.

Where does this information get us? Paul speaks of mankind in Acts 17, "27 That they should seek the Lord, if haply they might feel after him, and find him, though he be not far from every one of us." How can God not be far from us if He is all the way in heaven? The answer is not a matter of third dimensional logistics, but of fourth, fifth, sixth, and seventh dimensional logistics. Jesus elaborates somewhat on this in John 4, "24 God is a Spirit: and they that worship him must worship him in spirit and in truth." God, a spirit, is able to interact within *and without* our existence in ways humanity cannot fully comprehend, due to the nature of God verses the nature of mankind. God is not just an inter-dimensional being, but perhaps better described as an *extra-dimensional* being, meaning, a being outside our dimensional influence. Looking up to heaven, one must look beyond the visible, into a multi-faceted creation which does not reside in the ethereal mindset of theologians, but nearby in the very places we walk and live. This must be what allows prayer to work. Our *physical* words and thoughts cannot go anywhere outside earshot. Only a *spiritual* word can do that.

Piecing things together, the spiritual realm is not necessarily a parallel dimension, but rather, a stacking of dimensions that intertwine with our own. These are not able to be perceived with our physical senses. The spiritual realm would likely have similar (if not the exact same) foundational laws that we experience ourselves. Albeit, in the spiritual realm, these same laws may manifest differently than we are used to experiencing. In all fairness, it seems that any endeavor to describe the spiritual realm would be tantamount to describing a cube, having only the drawing of a square with which to work. While not impossible to do, this is certainly not without its complications. For example, both squares and cubes have ninety-degree angles on a square face. However, when gravity is factored in on the mass of the objects, the cube would be impacted much more, due to density. Other aspects of three-dimensional existence would cause the cube's surface area to become an important factor with as well. In contrast, a square has little to no interaction with these problems in its two dimensional existence.

If the laws of this physical world are linked and expressed in the spirit, then one must look at creation with a broader perspective. The physical dimension would not be wildly different or obscure to the spirit, but merely a few steps down. Oddly enough, an excellent example of this is how people can be in two places at once. According to the Apostle Paul, God "6 hath raised us up together, and made us sit together in heavenly places in Christ Jesus" (Ephesians 2:6). What Paul is saying is not a physical co-existence, but a spiritual one. A reality such as this would normally break the laws of Newtonian physics. Yet, in quantum super-positioning, it becomes possible with information and possibly physical things (Fein, 2019). Paul is not speaking of a physical presence in heaven, but that people can have a spiritual presence in heaven and a physical presence on Earth, an example of quantum entanglement. Two objects, in two different places, are able to share information without physical contact. As Einstein put it, "spooky stuff at a distance."

Looking at the supernatural in a wider scope may help explain some difficult concepts, such as the trinity of God and how the Holy Spirit can interact in our lives. More so, it illustrates how Jesus Christ and the Father can be within Christians and still be in "Heaven" at the same time. In John 15 and 16, Jesus describes the mystery of God making His abode in us: how He is the vine and we are the branches. Jesus chooses this particular terminology to expand our understanding of God and the spiritual realm.

On a parallel topic, two questions that may be raised are: 1) How big is God? 2) How small is the earth? If NASA photos are any indication, the earth is a tiny, microscopic spec in a sea of stars. A true wonder to behold. In many ways, this view of Earth is not unlike how a bacteria may appear to a person. Or even more so, how a human embryo may begin life as only a single cell within its mother. Even so, a view of one of the trillions of cells present in our own bodies is not too distant a comparison. If one were to look at a single cell from space, it goes without saying it would not be visible. Yet, God is aware of it. The nucleus of a human cell, which contains the DNA, is even smaller still. Of course, it is well known that the complexities of life continue to amaze humanity the closer we look. Without a doubt, God is attempting to teach humanity something.

While there are likely innumerable concepts that can be (and have been) extracted from examining the intricacies of life, there is another theme worth exploring in tandem: fractals. A fractal is a concept of something that, regardless of its size, scale, or format, if one zooms into the medium, it will not look entirely different than if one were to zoom out. This is easily demonstrated in a mesmerizing spiral of color. The spiral can be expanded, or shrunk, but the effect is the same. A spiral is by nature, a fractal. Another example of fractals which appear naturally is the sphere surrounded by water. The earth at the time of creation followed this format, where the firmament divided the waters from the waters. The same shape: a globe with an exterior of water based material, is seen in the human cell and its membrane; and in the womb, with the water lining protecting the unborn child.

What is so important about water covering globes? It may just sound like God approves of squishy bouncy balls. However, when plugging in the ideas of water in the Bible, such as baptism, there arises a deeper point of view. Admittedly, this is an incomplete picture, but consider for a moment that all these things were created by God for a particular purpose. As an engineer, God made similarities within His designs. What's more however, God created everything with a particular purpose and logical teaching element for humanity. Perhaps, God wished to explain His viewpoint of mankind, by creating smaller models people can interact with. An embryo in a mother's womb, a tiny working cell among millions of others, or an earth seemingly insignificant in a sea of galaxies, quite reminiscent of Psalm 8, "what is man that thou art mindful of Him?"

The fact that God came as Jesus Christ shows He is very mindful of us. Again, John 3:16 witnesses to God's love of the *cosmos*. Jesus mentions in the Gospels how not even a sparrow falls without God's notice (Matthew 10:29-31). The beautiful old hymn, *His eye is on the Sparrow* is based on this reference. God, being above a huge sea of stars, focuses on the earth. The earth is enormous, yet even the tiny birds are accounted for alongside human beings as individuals, among our many billions. Although the earth is minute in scale compared to the universe, it is even smaller in comparison to God. The question remains to be answered however, "How big is God?" As discussed above, God inhabits eternity. Eternity is outside the third heaven, which is itself outside space. Space is huge. It is epic in scale and majesty; an artist's canvas and an engineer's marvel. A true testament to God's innate character and abilities. Yet, in all of outer-space's marvel, it lacks a level of intricacy. That intricacy has only been observed in living creations.

A single cell is more complicated than the working of an entire galaxy. The stars run on circuits which are hardly ever interrupted. A cell on the other hand, must respond to an ever changing environment, exhibiting a level of vastly superior intelligence. Cells contain power stations, a central government, and an advanced infrastructure system that would be the envy of any city on the planet. Stars and galaxies, on the other hand, do none of these things. It is almost as if God built things in reverse. Instead of using simple things to build complex systems (like people usually do), God uses complex systems to build simple things. Humans built computers the size of small buildings at first, then eventually were able to miniaturize them into handheld devices. Even these are made up of ever simpler parts and pieces. While a great deal of intricacy is evident in electronics, these items are not used as basic materials to construct larger things. The Pyramids and the Great Wall are not made of smart phones. They are only made of rocks; polished and formed rocks, but rocks, nonetheless. This is where the idiom, "the whole is more than the sum of its parts" emanates.

The parts and pieces humans create are simple, but together make something more complex. God on the other hand, uses cells (extremely complex systems) to create a body (a comparatively simple system). A robot is a mechanical body with a computerized mind, but no robot can ever do what the human body can. A human body (as a body) could never do what a single cell within it does. But the body is necessary to interact with the world God created. The Apostle Paul explains some of this discrepancy in I Corinthians 7:27, "God hath chosen the foolish things of the world to confound the wise; and God hath chosen the weak things of the world to confound the things which are mighty."

While the strength of mankind tends to dictate its path, God has chosen to showcase a sense of humility in His creation. God, instead of creating things in a way that mankind would, instead chose to do it the opposite way. In this sense, it requires humanity to look beyond the obvious and rely more on their Creator, and couples very strongly with the Beatitudes spoken by Jesus Christ in Matthew 5:

"3 Blessed are the poor in spirit: for theirs is the kingdom of heaven. 4 Blessed are they that mourn: for they shall be comforted. 5 Blessed are the meek: for they shall inherit the earth. 6 Blessed are they which do hunger and thirst after righteousness: for they shall be filled. 7 Blessed are the merciful: for they shall obtain mercy. 8 Blessed are the pure in heart: for they shall see God. 9 Blessed are the peacemakers: for they shall be called the children of God. 10 Blessed are they which are persecuted for righteousness' sake: for theirs is the kingdom of heaven."

The universe, with its complex simplicity, displays plainly in both the grandiose and minute natures, that God is a God of both the *macro* and *micro* realms. God is a masterful designer who is invested in the big picture and a caring Father who is involved in the little things of life as well.

CHAPTER 3

Did Creation Happen as Described in the Bible?

Having already explored multiple evidences contained within the universe which point to God, there is ample opportunity to examine the creation story as outlined in Genesis chapters 1 and 2. Much debate exists regarding this topic in reference to Evolution Theory, Constant-State Theory and others. While there is clear evidence that the universe had a beginning (discussed previously), many Christians have since compromised their faith, in order not to appear unscientific. In short, God has been moved aside to make room for someone (or something) else in many Christian's minds. By itself this is worrisome, because that is exactly what the devil attempts to do in every aspect of life.

Respect ought to be given scientists in their individual fields, as they offer a great service to society. Without scientific quandaries, forward progress is slowed. Scientific research is a wonderful endeavor and has improved the quality of life for billions of people across the globe. That being said, science has little, or nothing to do with religion in its basic form. Science is about understanding the physical world, whereas religion is meant to explain it's origins and hidden workings from a spiritual perspective. What's more, many of the individuals dedicated to the fields of Evolution (with which Creation Theory is the largest contender) are self-proclaimed atheists. Although there is a growing number of evolution touting monotheists, the vast majority in the fields of question are not. The fact that the majority of the opposition to Creationism is founded in Atheism is very telling.

A puzzling conundrum emerges from the apparent division between science and religion. Religion in its pure form is unadulterated truth (or belief of truth), which may, or may not, be based on facts. If all the religions of the world were scrambled together (as some attest to doing) then a muddy conglomerate of nonsense emerges. Religions cannot agree with one another on basic doctrines and while many theologies contest that humans ought to treat one another well, the reasonings behind each belief system vary so widely that they cannot be reconciled. Monotheism on the other hand, stands out from other religious paradigms. The three *main* monotheistic religions happen to all be based on the Bible: Judaism, Christianity, and Islam. These three contest that there is only one God, and they all agree in the same creation story as outlined in Genesis. What is more, the only religious groups which attest to defending their creation story with any real validity, belong to these three. The fact that an argument exists between the Biblical creation story and scientific reasoning (largely in the form of evolution) makes bare the uncertainty upon which certain scientific paradigms are based.

Science is designed to be changed and modified as new information emerges. Science, by nature is not concrete, but moldable. This is due to the understanding that new knowledge will always arise. Many scientific hypotheses, and even some laws, have been challenged and reversed due to newer discoveries. An excellent example is the aether: a force throughout the universe thought to be too subtle to be felt, but exhibited force on everything. Its presence would only be noticed over long periods of time and at large distances (such as with galactic movements). The novel idea was first touted by Newton in his book *Opticks: A Treatise of the Reflexions, Refractions, Inflexions and Colours of Light*, published in 1704. However, some two-hundred years later, the coffin for the aether was sealed by Einstein's theory of relativity. Einstein posited explanations to universal behaviors without the need for the aether, and his position is substantiated by mathematics. Nevertheless, some recent research into quantum mechanics and dark matter have revitalized the fundamental idea of the aether (Townsend, 2022). The fact that science is able to do such a double back on itself is proof of both its flexibility and fallibility.

Religion, on the other hand, is far more rigid. Due to this dichotomy in natures between science and religion, logic would dictate that such changing scientific theories ought to move about the statutes governing the Biblical creation. Why should this be? Because the Scriptures claim to be an eyewitness account. If Scripture did not make this claim, then proof of its veracity is superfluous. However, since the Bible claims to be true, and no one on Earth was there at the time, then a reasonable assumption to its truth should be considered. As to date, no sufficient evidence has surfaced which removes the Bible from the playing field. In fact, the majority of new evidence coming to light reinforces the Biblical narrative and reignites the controversy. Therefore, it is incumbent upon Christians to reflect Biblical truth in their viewpoints, rather than denominational/doctrinal "truth."

The conflict between denominational doctrine and Biblical truth boils down to the main cornerstone of this text: humility. There is no need for this text to explore the meat and potatoes evidence governing the Creation model and accompanying arguments. A great number of faith-filled scientists and theologians have already trodden that ground effectively enough to warrant one's trust in the Holy Writ. Thoughts will be deposited here and beliefs brief, so as to better steep within the minds of the audience. Each person must, regardless of the evidence laid before them, must make their own, personal choices regarding the validity of the Word of God. As such, they must give account for their beliefs, not only to their family and peers, but ultimately to God Himself at the end. There is wisdom in accepting what God says at the expense of human philosophers, rather than taking the word of human philosophers at the expense of God.

Genesis chapter 1 clearly states a literal six day creation. In fact, six, twenty-four hour days in multiple cases. The Hebrew is precise. The logic of this is sound also, with the differences in time between plants, the sun, and pollinators. The symbiosis of creation would not work had its components not been simultaneously instituted. The days could not be long days (millions of years as some purport) or else the plants would have ceased to exist and the animals would have nothing to eat when they came onto the scene. Mankind has derived aging methods for the earth and the universe which are tempting to include in the Biblical narrative. The vast majority of said inventors are well intentioned and more knowledgeable than others outside their fields of research. It would be foolish however, to assert that in God's book He doesn't know what He is talking about. The question then becomes, wherein lies the mistake?

Most modern dating methods rely on the assumption that the way things are now, have always been. When Noah's flood enters the equation, this base assumption loses validity. Carl Baugh's Creation model displays a world where the earth was so different and intricate that nothing of it still exists (Bassett, 2011). The Apostle Peter asserts in II Peter 3:6 that, "6... the world that then was, being overflowed with water, perished." The scale of the flood, and the destruction caused by it is unparalleled to anything which has ever occurred on the earth. In fact, it's unparalleled to anything that will happen, short of the great cataclysms found in the Book of Revelation.

In light of this, it would be shortsighted to assert that the world looks relatively like it did at the time of creation. The millions of tons of fossil fuels showcase the level of destruction into which the previous world fell. The depth at which these materials are mined, reveals the sheer amount of earth deposited by the great alluvial catastrophe.

The Bible is plain on its reading. God is capable of a miraculous creation, otherwise He wouldn't be God. Though, God *could* have used Evolution too. He is *all-powerful* after all. Many assert a combination of Evolution with Scripture to account for the differences in our timeline. There is one thing though that needs to be pointed out: the creation account in the Bible is clearly meant to be read from the position of God, not the position of mankind. If one were to apply some of Einstein's Theory of Relativity, then it's possible (almost certain in fact) that God experiences and views time differently than we do. In fact, Gerald Schroeder asserts this idea in his book *Genesis One*, where he explores the implications of universal expansion and our viewpoint of time. In another way, in terms of creation, God is looking forward, whereas humanity is looking backward.

If one struggles with the creation of the universe by God as a miraculous event, then perhaps one should look into the validity of the resurrection of Jesus Christ. His resurrection is not only historically substantiated, but in many ways an even more miraculous event than the creation. Why? Because the creation happened from without the universe, with God inputting His power. In contrast, God came as the man Jesus Christ, who became subject to the very laws He made (John 1:1-14). Within these very laws God functioned to be raised from the dead, contrary to even the devil himself. The Apostle Paul states in I Corinthians 2:8b, "for had [the devils] known [of the mystery of God], they would not have crucified the Lord of glory."

Would a God capable of resurrecting Himself against all the odds really leave the universe to be a "self-starter" for eons of time? The resurrection was instantaneous! Could not God create the earth and the rest of the universe in an instant? He says He did. Therefore it seems reasonable to assume that humanity has an issue with its perceptions of the universe, rather than God being a liar. Regardless of doctrinal position, it is up to the individual to either believe what God says, or not. Belief in the literal six-day creation is important, because it has the potential to show that either God is all-powerful, or He isn't. Either God can work miracles, or He can't. Either He rose from the dead, or He didn't.

CHAPTER 4

What is the State of Mankind?

Humanity has always pondered certain questions surrounding life and the universe. Each religion in the world, including Atheism and Secular Humanism, attempts to answer them. The questions are:

1. Who am I?
2. What am I doing here?
3. How did I get here?
4. Where am I going when I die?

Every civilization in history has given an answer to these fundamental questions (or their variants). The title of this chapter is a coalescence of those ponderings listed above and brings into focus a related query: What is an individual's standing with God? If this can be answered, it will help resolve other related dilemmas. Of course, when one studies the Bible, more inquiries present themselves, for example: 1) Are people born with a sin nature? 2) If so, how did it come about? 3) What does a sin nature even mean? 4) Couldn't God simply have forgiven us and not required that Jesus die? 5) Why did Jesus have to be born as a man (mankind)? These topics will need to be explored to uncover the system God created and to understand why He made it the way He did.

One of the first things to notice about the questions above is that they are actually legal in nature. All questions having to do with the fundamental laws of the universe, including people and sin, have a lawful, legal connection. This is due in part because of something Paul speaks of in Romans 8, called "the law of sin and death," in contrast to "the law of life in Christ Jesus." There are many laws God ordained at the beginning of creation to govern the universe (laws governing gravity, mathematics, and chemistry are well known examples). Beyond physical laws however, there are unseen laws which govern consciousness and thought, as well as emotions and so forth. While some aspects of these laws have physical connections, such as our brains, there are aspects beyond the physical realm.

The law of sin and death did not take effect immediately at the beginning of creation, like the other laws mentioned above. The law of sin and death took effect in creation when Adam willfully ate of the fruit, in full disobedience to God's command. It is an important distinction however, that the knowledge of good and evil, from eating the fruit of the tree, wasn't the sin. The sin was the disobedience involved of eating from the tree when expressly forbidden. God's judgment afterwards brought the law of sin and death into effect as a consequence of Adam's willful disobedience. Moreover, Adam's insubordination gave place to the devil (the serpent) in his and his descendants' lives.

Going back to how Paul described the law of sin in Romans 7 and 8, it is reminiscent of laws governing slavery in Leviticus. While these passages have been largely analyzed in light of Roman culture, it would seem inopportunistic to ignore the Mosaic connections. To understand slavery in a Biblical context, one must understand its causes and implications. Slavery in the Torah is split along a few different lines, but the main focus for this purpose will be the difference between Israelites and non-Israelites. Exodus 20, Leviticus 25, and Deuteronomy 15 cover this topic in detail.

An important point to make is that each of the above passages deals with a level of nuance in the Mosaic law and may not necessarily be dealing with the exact same law in writing. The Torah was written, not as a legalistic document in the modern sense, but rather uses real life examples to explain spiritual laws. These generalized spiritual laws were meant to be understood by the priests, who acted as judges. Just because a sin was technically missing from the Torah, doesn't mean it was sanctioned. It was still against the spirit of the law. Paul echoes this in Romans 8. Such fundamental understanding of the Torah in general is very critical for the application of these concepts dealing with mankind. Furthermore, it is essential that this fundamental idea be synthesized, in order to expand one's understanding of how God thinks and relates to humanity in general.

Moving to the nuts and bolts of slavery in Mosaic law, it is easiest to begin with native born Israelites. Israelites who were in poor economic conditions could sell themselves into a form of indentured servitude. This may have been done, for example, to pay off one's debts. If the debt was owed to a particular individual (i.e., a loan, or repayment of stolen goods) then the debt would be considered paid after 6 years of service. However, when the debt was due to exterior forces (such as poor crop yields causing a red-line in the GDP), then an Israelite could sell his land rights and ultimately himself into slavery. In the latter case, the Hebrew and any direct family members would go out free in the year of Jubilee (once every fifty years). When the time of servitude was completed, he could choose, instead of taking his freedom, to submit to his master in lifelong service. This action would subjugate himself, and any future children born under that servitude, to remain as slaves.

Non-Israelites did not have the same rights as native Israelites and were not released in the year of Jubilee. For ease of understanding, this would be the common type of slavery seen throughout world history. Non-Israelites could find themselves in a state of slavery through a multitude of circumstances. Warfare was the most common avenue for attaining slaves, seconded by international slave markets at the time. Interestingly enough, Exodus 21:16 submits that the punishment for unlawfully kidnapping someone and selling them into slavery is death. The passage here highlights a concept that slavery should only occur to an individual through their own actions and choices. Even when servitude is required as a recourse for a crime, such as paying back the cost of stolen goods, it is from that individual's own direct actions that the slavery is caused.

How this relates to the state of mankind is profound. Adam in the fall, committed a legal crime. In God's court it was a secular, as well as religious, transgression. The punishment for the crime was sin and death. As Adam was sold into slavery under this law of sin and death and unable to pay the price, he was incapable of securing freedom by his own hand. Due to the nature of the criminal act, servitude was mandated by God as the proper recourse, and as such, Adam would not be freed at the year of Jubilee. He would be freed when the debt was paid. In consequence, all children born while in the servitude (slavery) would remain the property of the master (Exodus 21:3-4). The master in this case is not a person, but a law: the law of sin and death.

As all mankind (or Adam-kind) resulted from Adam and Eve, their children remain the property of sin. The slave "caste" system is perpetuated and inescapable in God's courtroom, because we do not belong to ourselves. We are not free born. Mankind is unable to individually pay the necessary price for freedom, even through death, because each person has sinned. While people are not born guilty, they are born with a sin nature. The physical body (i.e., the flesh) is subject to the law of sin and death. Subjectivity to sin and death results in the sin oozing out in daily life and corrupting each and every individual in their own slurry of godlessness. As Paul states in Romans 3:23, "For all have sinned and fallen short of the glory of God." However, possibilities for redemption exist, as Leviticus 25:47-49 states:

"47... And if a sojourner or stranger wax rich by thee, and thy brother that dwelleth by wax poor, and sell himself unto the stranger or sojourner by thee, or to the stock of the stranger's family: 48 After that he is sold he may be redeemed again; one of his brethren may redeem him: 49 Either his uncle, or his uncle's son, may redeem him, or any that is nigh of kin unto him of his family may redeem him; or if he is able, he may redeem himself."

Despite the potential for redemption, people are unable to redeem themselves, or one another from sin. Only a man who had lived a sinless life could be a candidate for paying the price and redeeming another. The only way to live a sinless life though, would be to be born without a sin nature. This is impossible unless God Himself were to intervene. Here is why Paul in I Corinthians 15:45-49 describes the Lord Jesus Christ as the "second man," or the "second Adam" as it were. Earlier, in verse 22 Paul states, "For as in Adam all die, even so in Christ shall all be made alive." Only God Himself, as the man Jesus Christ, could redeem us from sin. That is why Jesus had to be all God, and all man, not half and half. All and all, that he might become all in all (I Corinthians 15:28). In this way, Jesus is nearest of kin to us. Not the exact same, but similar enough to be considered "next of kin," making Him eligible to redeem us. Of course, the price necessary to purchase humanity was death. Jesus, willfully, offered Himself, as He said in John 10:18, "18 No man taketh [my life] from me, but I lay it down of myself. I have power to lay it down, and I have power to take it again. This commandment have I received of my Father."

Jesus gave up His own life in order to pay each individual's sin debt, being our kinsman-redeemer. The debt was not His own, but He chose to bring us out of bondage. Jesus had to willfully give Himself up, because He was making a conscious choice to use His life as a payment for our transgressions. Jesus' statement in John 15:13, "13 Greater love hath no man than this, that a man lay down his life for his friends" bears out this point. We no longer belong to the stranger of sin and death that has ruled over us; but instead, we were granted our freedom by the Son of God who loved us and gave Himself for us. The Old Testament book of Ruth recorded Boaz redeeming Ruth to be his wife; likewise Christ redeemed the Church to be His bride. Paul explains this more fully in Galatians 4:3-7:

"3 Even so we, when we were children, were in bondage under the elements of the world: 4 But when the fullness of the time was come, God sent forth his Son, made of a woman, made under the law, 5 To redeem them that were under the law, that we might receive the adoption of sons. 6 And because ye are sons, God hath sent forth the Spirit of his Son into your hearts, crying, Abba, Father. 7 Wherefore thou art no more a servant, but a son; and if a son, then an heir of God through Christ."

A question which naturally comes at this point is one that plagues many: if Jesus redeemed mankind from the law of sin and death, then why do people still sin? The adoption spoken of by Paul means that Jesus Christ created a whole new genealogy, separate from the lineage of Adam. People may be grafted into the new genealogy as part of the new covenant. It is not through the flesh, but through the spirit (John 1:12-13). Jesus explains this to Nicodemus in John 3:1-21 when he says, "Except a man be born again, he cannot see the kingdom of God." While Nicodemus points out that being born again physically is impossible, "Jesus answered, Verily, verily, I say unto thee, Except a man be born of water and of the Spirit, he cannot enter into the kingdom of God. 6 That which is born of the flesh is flesh; and that which is born of the Spirit is spirit."

Paul echoes the words of Christ in Romans 8, "1 There is therefore now no condemnation to them which are in Christ Jesus, who walk not after the flesh, but after the Spirit. 2 For the law of the Spirit of life in Christ Jesus hath made me free from the law of sin and death. 3 For what the law could not do, in that it was weak through the flesh, God sending his own Son in the likeness of sinful flesh, and for sin, condemned sin in the flesh: 4 That the righteousness of the law might be fulfilled in us, who walk not after the flesh, but after the Spirit."

Therefore, there is a new birth which is tangible, yet only attainable by grace, through faith in Jesus Christ alone. It can only begin with the covering of the blood of the Lamb, shed on Calvary (Hebrews 9:22). This new birth and life exist alongside the old. While the old is dying, the new is continuously living through the power of the resurrected Lord. Paul explores this dual nature of Christians in Romans 7, "14 For we know that the law is spiritual: but I am carnal, sold under sin." Paul recognizes the *fleshly* nature of humanity is not "born again," but through Christ, the *spiritual* nature is "born again." In this, our fleshly nature (physical being) is still subject to the law of sin and death. That is why people still die physically and moreover, why people still sin. Christ did not come to redeem our fallen, sinful, physical bodies. He came to call us to a new life and resurrection (Luke 5:37-39, II Corinthians 5, and Revelation 21).

Paul continues in Romans 7 by relating his own experiences with the sin nature. His account is applicable to many Christians who have battled sin in their lives. "15 For that which I do I allow not: for what I would, that do I not; but what I hate, that do I. 16 If then I do that which I would not, I consent unto the law that it is good. 17 Now then it is no more I that do it, but sin that dwelleth in me." While Paul is talking in the context of Mosaic law, it is important to remember the overarching truths he is pointing out. Although Christians are not under the Mosaic law (Christ made a new covenant), the spiritual law of sin and death is still very active. It is this spiritual law that is important to keep in mind as Paul speaks.

Paul communicatesthe duality of natures within a Christian. It is pivotal to recall that Paul is not speaking on his own, but is divulging truths which were given to him by God Himself. It is therefore not what Paul thinks, but what God thinks; albeit, Paul is using his own experiences to make the point. Put another way, many addicts may describe their actions in a similar way Paul does here in Romans 7; a *desire* not to fulfill their craving, but still a *behavior* which does. The instinct overpowers the reasoning. What Paul states, beginning with verse 21, is intriguing:

"21 I find then a law, that, when I would do good, evil is present with me. 22 For I delight in the law of God after the inward man: 23 But I see another law in my members, warring against the law of my mind, and bringing me into captivity to the law of sin which is in my members. 24 O wretched man that I am! who shall deliver me from the body of this death? 25 I thank God through Jesus Christ our Lord. So then with the mind I myself serve the law of God; but with the flesh the law of sin."

When diving into the aspects of God on issues as sticky as sin, it becomes important to understand the legal aspects in God's courtroom. When Christ died on the cross and redeemed us, He created a new covenant (contract) with us, which was prophesied in Jeremiah 31:31-34:

"31 Behold, the days come, saith the Lord, that I will make a new covenant with the house of Israel, and with the house of Judah: 32 Not according to the covenant that I made with their fathers in the day that I took them by the hand to bring them out of the land of Egypt; which my covenant they brake, although I was an husband unto them, saith the Lord: 33 But this shall be the covenant that I will make with the house of Israel; After those days, saith the Lord, I will put my law in their inward parts, and write it in their hearts; and will be their God, and they shall be my people. 34 And they shall teach no more every man his neighbour, and every man his brother, saying, Know the Lord: for they shall all know me, from the least of them unto the greatest of them, saith the Lord: for I will forgive their iniquity, and I will remember their sin no more."

That is the New Covenant made between God and mankind, if we accept the sacrifice of the Lord Jesus Christ. While Israel was offered the New Covenant originally, they rejected the Messiah which brought it; and the Covenant (or contract) was instead given to the Gentiles (Deuteronomy 29:21, Ephesians 3, Romans 9). While we are not to continue living in sin (Romans 6), God is gracious to work with us. As John says in I John 1:9, "9 If we confess our sins, he is faithful and just to forgive us our sins, and to cleanse us from all unrighteousness."

The cleansing can only happen through the work of the Lord in one's life. Notice the last part of I John 1:9 indicates the cleansing is done by God. Recall also in Acts 10 (when Peter was sent to Cornelius, a Gentile), "What God hath cleansed, that call not thou common." Therefore, if God is the one cleansing, then He is the judge of what is clean or unclean. Not the individual being cleaned. This is of course a process (i.e. sanctification). While, however, there is "no condemnation to them which are in Christ Jesus" the next part is often forgotten, "who walk not after the flesh, but after the Spirit" (Romans 8). It remains imperative therefore to be continuously walking after the Spirit. In this way, we are able to partake of the graciousness of God.

Walking in the Spirit may be considered "a work" by some, but God does not view it in the same way people do. In truth, God does not just love people as they are, but loves us more than that. God loves us so much, that He doesn't want to leave us in the state of sin where He found us. God wants to lift us up, to stand where He stands, and to sit where He sits. "Blessed are they which are called unto the marriage supper of the Lamb" (Revelation 19:9).

God does not expect perfection in an imperfect world. God does expect growth however. He is very understanding, forgiving, and realistic. He does not hold people accountable for things they are not yet ready to handle. When He brings people to a certain point in their life, He does expect them to move beyond old worldly views and habits and take on the new nature instead. Israel during the Exodus journey, was expected to follow through as God hopes for us now; however, Israel as a nation never did. Here, the parable of the seeds in Matthew 13 comes to mind. Seeds are planted so that they grow and produce a crop. If a seed never grows, then it is wasted. If a Christian never grows, then the blood of Christ was made vain in their life. The blood of Christ and the Holy Spirit are what God has used to plant His vineyard. He is the vine; we are the branches. John 15:2, "2 Every branch in me that beareth not fruit he taketh away: and every branch that beareth fruit, he purgeth it, that it may bring forth more fruit."

New life through Jesus Christ starts small. However, as God's Spirit is magnified within the heart of the individual, He takes over aspects of their lives. This may be piece by piece, thought by thought, but it does happen in a tangible way. God is too big a God, to enter one's heart and not provoke changes in the person's life. The Christian walk is like crossing a wide river, navigating the rocks which protrude from the water, to reach the other side. Each rock is a steppingstone in the Christian life, which God brings up, or changes, that result in the growth of the individual. Each step brings them closer to God in divine intimacy. The stones are different sizes, with some taking longer to traverse than others, but the individual strives to cross nonetheless. If they slip and fall, they get wet and perhaps sustain injuries, but then stand up and continue their journey.

The only time a Christian would find him or herself truly falling short (sin) would be if he or she decided to camp-out and proceed no further, thus in effect, refusing to cross the river. Put another way, they fall short of the goal and "miss the mark." The Pharisees in the Gospels were in this situation. Despite what Jesus taught them, they preferred to 'camp-out' on their *perceptions* of truth. Had they truly known and believed the Scriptures, they would have continued to 'cross the river,' by accepting Jesus as the Messiah. With regards to the individual Christian, these obstacles can vary widely. Regardless of their size or composition however, God will lead the person through, to the end (I Corinthians 10:13). After all, He is the "author and finisher of our faith" (Hebrews 12:2).

CHAPTER 5

What is the Fear of the LORD?

"The fear of the Lord" is a phrase encountered from time to time when reading the Bible. What does this phrase mean and how should it impact Christians? Are Christians meant to be afraid of God? Afraid of Jesus? Most people think of fear as some horrendous emotion tied to nail biting. It can come as suddenly as finding out you forgot someone's birthday or anniversary. There are of course deeper and harsher types of fear tied to traumatic situations. PTSD comes from heavy experiences of fear (and stress) and can impact a person's psyche for years. However, there is also a fear tied to reverence. Most people familiar with this topic will understand the idea of reverence as being how the fear of the LORD is commonly interpreted. That being said, there is a distinct activity tied to fear which is often missed.

The topic of fear is frequently an area where people get into trouble. Not only do many people in Western society struggle with anxiety and depression, but there is a distinct subculture tied to fear and death. Horror movies for example and many of the celebrations which occur during Halloween, revolve around fear. There are portions of Western culture with appear to glorify fear. This is not the fear God is speaking of in the Scriptures. To expand on the topic of "the fear of the LORD," the general subject of fear will need to be explored.

First and foremost, the King James Version of the Bible was written in a different time period. As a result, words were often understood in a different fashion, just as in the Hebrew and Greek texts of the Scriptures. Not only has English changed over time, but the nuance of words used can, and do, have different meanings to various audiences and cultures. An example would be how the words gay, cool, and weed have changed due to cultural usage. The words themselves translate into any other language as "happy," "not hot," and "invasive plant." Without cultural context, their meanings become muddled. In the past, when monarchies were the common form of government, a different disposition existed between the ruler and the subjects. How this relationship was perceived was written into the dedication of the KJV to King James in 1611 (most Authorized versions still retain it). It refers to King James as "our most dread sovereign." Were the translators afraid of their heads being chopped off by the King? Possibly, but not likely. Here can be seen how the concept of fear is used in a way different than most. It conveys an idea of reverence, as well as power. In the old English (and in abstract concept nowadays) the words fear, dread, and afraid, all have to do with the *placement* of power. More specifically, the *acknowledgment* of power.

In modern times, fear has been defined more as a condition, or emotion. Fear is thought of as passive; almost like finding oneself hungry or thirsty. In the past however, fear, and some emotions in general, were considered less situational and more proactive. Likewise, a similar difference can be seen in the words joy and happiness. Happiness is related to the word happenstance, meaning: the happiness of the individual is relative to the conditions in which one is found. Joy on the other hand, is not subject to conditions; it is in fact a noun. Joy is something someone has, or does not have, but it is not subject to the environment. Different than happiness, joy is attained by an individual and *retained*, as long as they hold onto it. As Christians, our joy is a positive exuberance based on who Jesus is, rather than who we are or what is happening around us (Psalm 51:12). Contrary however to joy and happiness, fear is actually a verb. While joy and happiness vary in their root definitions, they are still both passive by themselves. Fear on the other hand, denotes action. To be afraid is an adjective, but to fear is a verb. It is not passive, but active. If one is afraid, it is because they fear something. The adjective follows the verb. This important distinction will help to shed light on the different types of fear and what is actually going on when a person fears something.

In exploring fear as an action, it is no secret that fear is often tied to danger, or more precisely, power. When one is afraid, that person is looking at the power something else has over them, whether held by a person or a circumstance. Fear however may be muted or diminished in stressful situations. Seasoned soldiers, for example, may not experience excessive fear of their enemy due to bullet-proof gear and armored vehicles. If one has a good spouse or friend, there is less need to fear the fact that an important date was forgotten. It does not mean there is no apprehension, but the strength of the relationship (like armor) can protect against mishaps. Perhaps an even better example is the fear of losing a job with its potential avalanche of unfortunate events. The fear experienced by these individuals (being in combat or losing their job) comes from an outside force, beyond their control.

A lottery also serves the construct of looking at powers beyond a person: someone buys a lottery ticket, in the hopes of winning, based on the potential power the ticket holds. The anticipation and anxiety felt when the numbers are read off can be exhilarating, similar to waiting for the winning BINGO number to be called with each roll of the ball reel. The individual with a lottery ticket (or a nearly full BINGO card) is fearing what the results will be. The term fear can be applied, because the individual is looking at the potential power, beyond themselves, that could have a significant impact on them: either if they win, or, the anxiety if they lose.

The concept of the lottery ticket and BINGO balls envelope an emotion. A similar emotion can be felt at a sports game. It is hard to imagine a soccer game without the cheering and chants of the audience. Where does the emotion of the crowd come from? There is a big concoction of feeling throughout a game's progression. Yet, when a crowd jeers and boos and cries out against the referees, it is because they want what is best for their team. As a consequence, the emotion is tied to the audience looking at a particular target and responding to the situation from that viewpoint. When the target becomes threatened, then anger and disgust can erupt. When the target appears attainable, then elation and cheers break out. One's fear is the active choice to look at the target, while emotional ties follow in response. Any doubt about this can be resolved by finding people who care nothing about soccer and asking how they felt during the World Cup. The answer will likely be that they didn't feel anything. Why? Because they weren't looking at the same target as everyone else around them. They were not afraid when players got injured or referees made bad calls. In fact, uninterested persons are not fazed a bit by anything that happens during a game, because they are not holding the same mindset a raucous crowd does. These concepts could be applied to a Christian's walk with God. It is true, individuals should have a fear of what God might do if they misbehave. The great white throne judgment at the end of time ought to have everyone in apprehension. However, if one accepts the Lord Jesus Christ as Messiah, then that person is covered by the blood of the Lamb and is no longer condemned in their trespasses. The fear of God's eternal wrath then has no power.

Beyond the obvious fear of God's wrath is a further understanding for life. As Solomon says in Proverbs 9:10, "The fear of the LORD is the beginning of wisdom." While it may appear initially that wisdom and fear are unrelated, Solomon is saying, if one wishes to be wise, one must learn to look at God's power influencing the world and one's own life. Thus, the fearing of the LORD, being a verb, an action, is an active thing people must do. By doing things with God in mind, individuals will begin to learn His way, which is His wisdom. Psalm 23 speaks of the Lord leading us in His "paths of righteousness" for His name's sake. The "paths of righteousness" spoken of by David are God's leading and directives in the life of a saint. If, however, saints do not acknowledge

God's power and influence, they will fall short of His plan for their lives. Falling short is the definition of sin.

Retaining the fear of the LORD is an ongoing process. Many things in life continually seek to move our attention away from God and toward the world. Peter and his companions experienced this in Acts 5:27-29 when they were reprimanded by Jewish authorities while preaching the Gospel. They responded however, "we ought to obey God rather than men." Peter and the others did not look at the power the Jewish authorities had over them, but rather the power God had in raising Jesus Christ up from the grave. A similar focus ("fear") is seen when Peter is beckoned by Jesus to walk on the sea of Galilee. As long as Peter kept his eyes on Jesus, he could walk on the power of Jesus' Word: "Come." However, when Peter looked at the power of the storm, he began to fear it rather than the power of Jesus' Words and started to sink (Mark 14:22-31).

Even if God does not wish someone to walk on water physically, He does expect people to overcome things in their own hearts and lives. The things to be overcome can be many; Revelation chapters 2 and 3 record blessings of enormous value given to saints who overcome through the power of the resurrection of Jesus Christ. The ability to overcome things in life can only be achieved by focusing on God. Like Peter, when one looks at Jesus and His power, rather than the powers of this world and the desires of the flesh, then one can walk above the circumstances of life. Our actions are a physical representation of our beliefs. Fear is an active choice.

CHAPTER 6

Is God a Monarch?

Many times and in different ways, the Scriptures describe God as a ruler. The Apostle Paul continually refers to Jesus as the Lord Jesus Christ. "Lord" of course, denotes rulership. Jehovah, YHWH, God as He revealed Himself to Moses and Israel means "The Almighty One." Notice the use of *the*, instead of *an*. By using *the* definite article, the name Jehovah (often translated LORD in the KJV) conveys a sense of absolute exclusive authority. The name is God's way of showing that despite everything else in existence, He sits above it all. Nothing is higher than Him and everything is within His reach. In fact, taken with some of the other concepts already explored, the true might of God's power is not easy to comprehend. In a world where there are so many laws and regulations which govern daily life, a picture of God as a ruler bound by His own creation can be painted. In much the same way, Earthly rulers are bound in some measure by the laws passed by their legislative bodies. With the LORD however, thankfully, this isn't the case.

God sets up rules (such as Mosaic law), to which He binds Himself at times. The covenant relationship God made with Israel shows He was willing to bind Himself to them. We have the same opportunity through Jesus Christ. These covenants are always to our benefit. From God's point of view, He has nothing to gain by a human entering into covenant with Him. God already owns everything and caused everything to exist. He is the "self-existent one," the great I AM. Jesus displayed a power of God which had not been seen on the earth prior to His arrival. While Elijah and Elisha are notable for God working wonders through them, Jesus does so many more miracles, and a wider breadth of miracles that showcase the LORD's power. These miracles are outside the normal laws of the universe and call on higher laws in order to function. Jesus is the I AM. He says so in John 8:58, "Verily, verily, I say unto you, Before Abraham was, I am." Jesus is Jehovah.

Much can be examined by how God has revealed Himself throughout the Bible. His power is beyond comprehension: yet, with all His might, God still created powerful angels. If there is any doubt to this fact, rereading Revelation will refresh the memory. Many of the judgments are authorized by God, but carried out by angels: one who cast a coal to the earth in Revelation 8; and another angel who used a sickle to reap the earth in Revelation 14. King David saw an angel standing over Jerusalem to smite the city with a plague in I Chronicles 21:16. The fiery chariot which took Elijah up to heaven and the army which Elisha saw later on in II Kings, show that God has a very powerful retinue at His command.

Why then did God create angels to do things He could have done Himself? In the Exodus and Red Sea crossing, the miracles are more often described as occurring through God's direct provision. While the death angel is clearly described as an angel, the parting of the Red Sea is described as God blowing with His nostrils in Exodus 15. While it could be a poetic rendition of the story, the fact remains that the miracles are attributed to God directly. In a similar way, the miracles of Jesus Christ are attributed to Himself directly.

Taking this information together, a picture forms, showing God as a ruler who delegates authority to His subjects for specific tasks. The angels (or even Christians) to whom God delegates are fully capable of fulfilling the task commanded. When it comes to Christians (and people in general) there is a tendency to doubt God's ability to choose people correctly. Both Moses and Gideon come to mind as examples, who doubted God's confidence in their leadership abilities. However, God equips those He calls.

God follows a governing policy that gives Himself full discretionary authority at any time. Despite this, God couples this power with strong, personal, restraint. This restraint appears as God allows the natural laws and powers (physical and spiritual) to run creation largely uninterrupted. He has delegated the rudimentary cogs of His creation machine to work as He originally intended. However, nothing happens without His notice (Matthew 10:29). A logical conclusion would be that God gets "daily reports" of some kind and from these He makes further decisions. This is similar to a system of government with a strong executive branch. Within the executive, there are various departments and bureaus. These departments all must answer to the President, but the President tends to leave them alone, unless a problem arises or changes are warranted.

In God's government however, He isn't a President. God is a monarch. Perhaps better described as a despot, though that term has poor connotations. The Apostle Paul often describes himself as a servant, and the Lord Jesus Christ as His master. "Master" denotes complete authority. Tied to the meaning of Jehovah is "the God whose power is beyond all that is, was, or ever will be." As such, He is LORD of Paul's life and ought to be LORD of every Christian's life. The New Covenant which God made through the sacrifice and resurrection of the Lord Jesus Christ, is outlined in Hebrews 8 and was discussed some in a previous chapter. The significance of this passage is that it states in verse 11, "And they shall not teach every man his neighbor, and every man his brother, saying, know the Lord: for all shall know me, from the least to the greatest." When this passage is coupled with John 15:4-5, a marvelous picture emerges: "4 Abide in me, and I in you. As the branch cannot bear fruit of itself, except it abide in the vine; no more can ye, except ye abide in me. 5 I am the vine, ye are the branches: He that abideth in me, and I in him, the same bringeth forth much fruit: for without me ye can do nothing."

The New Covenant referenced in Hebrews 8 includes the outpouring of the Holy Spirit and the indwelling of God within us. While the Holy Spirit was still very present in the world prior to Pentecost, He was not as widely poured out. The New Covenant can be accepted by anyone who wishes to partake of God's holy nature. This is what Jesus meant in John 6:54-58 when He said:

"54 Whoso eateth my flesh, and drinketh my blood, hath eternal life; and I will raise him up at the last day. 55 For my flesh is meat indeed, and my blood is drink indeed. 56 He that eateth my flesh, and drinketh my blood, dwelleth in me, and I in him. 57 As the living Father hath sent me, and I live by the Father: so he that eateth me, even he shall live by me. 58 This is that bread which came down from heaven: not as your fathers did eat manna, and are dead: he that eateth of this bread shall live for ever."

Jesus makes a point to say later on in verse 63, "It is the spirit that quickeneth; the flesh profiteth nothing: the words that I speak unto you, they are spirit, and they are life." Being able to partake of the nature of God is a spiritual portion, not a physical portion. Jesus is very clear on this point. The Apostle Paul later echoes Jesus in Romans 8:6, "6 For to be carnally minded is death; but to be spiritually minded is life and peace." Again, the focus of God is always on pulling us out of a carnal, fleshly, worldly, human, mindset.

The privilege that has been extended to humanity is without comparison and is a mystery created by God. The New Covenant allows individual human beings to enter into a deep, personal, covenant relationship with the LORD God Almighty. Peter describes it in I Peter 1:12 as something "which things the angels desire to look into." The angels themselves are not allowed into the position God has determined for mankind. Although, God works with angels to fulfill various tasks, His desire for humanity is to have a deeper relationship with Him and work together building His Kingdom. That being said however, God does not micromanage. He has created a unique, streamlined form of bureaucracy. Contrary to mankind's bureaucracies, God utilizes individuals, who have been granted authority, to conduct business within His laws. These individuals (such as Michael the archangel) may have charge over various jurisdictions. For example, Michael is described in Daniel 10 as being Prince over the people of Israel. Gabriel however, only shows up in Scripture as a messenger. A clear distinction in duties, where both positions are very valuable, but very different.

In the same way God has used angels, He has also used priests and prophets. While people appear to be less receptive to the Lord's will, it does not diminish His desire to use us as vessels for His work. Here is an excellent example of God's discretionary authority, as He always picks the right tool for His job. Each and every saint in the Kingdom of Heaven has a part to play, just as the angels do. God is logical and doesn't do things frivolously. Paul speaks of this in I Corinthians 12 regarding the different parts of the body. Israel and the Christian Church are both witnesses of God on the earth. Our life choices, as Christians, are important, because we need to show the presence of the Lord Jesus Christ in our lives.

God is far too big to be in our lives and in our hearts without igniting change. This change is never demanded in Scripture: it is expected. The distinction is important. Jesus' parable in Matthew 25:14-30 of the three servants who were given talents, one, two, and five respectively, displays an expectation of growth and development in a Christian's life. The money given to each servant to steward is representative of the various things God puts in one's care. Adam was given the earth to steward and God taught him, beginning with a garden.

God expects growth in a Christian's life. This is not unreasonable; after all, when God planted the Garden of Eden, He expected the plants to continue growing. It didn't mean there wouldn't need to be some pruning and other work involved, but the expectation of God was that there would be a return on His investment. God planted trees in the garden so they would continue to produce fruit. He plants Himself into the hearts of everyone who accepts His New Covenant, yielding fruit in the life of each individual. God chose to tabernacle with us, as expressed in the meaning of Emmanuel "God with us" (Isaiah 7:14, Matthew 1:23). Notice, these are all things God does Himself; He doesn't leave them for angels to do for Him. While angels may be used as laborers in God's fields, these projects have God on the job site, directing the work.

Returning to the parable in Matthew 25, the emotion the master expresses at the end is in response to his expectations of the servants' actions. Toward the two prosperous servants, the master is joyful, because the servants proved their worth. Not only did these servants do what was necessary (the bare minimum), but they worked above and beyond on behalf of the master. But the third servant, who only *returned* the master's money, was met with a different response than the others:

"26 His lord answered and said unto him, Thou wicked and slothful servant, thou knewest that I reap where I sowed not, and gather where I have not strawed: 27 Thou oughtest therefore to have put my money to the exchangers, and then at my coming I should have received mine own with usury."

It is interesting to note the master is not demanding, but rather, bewildered and disappointed at the lack of the third servant's activity. The master even proposes a simple, baseline, activity that the servant did not do. There was a clear expectation that the first two servants understood, but the third one was clueless. The master in the parable is an example of God. Specifically, Jehovah, the Almighty One. God as the Despot: the Master. As a despot, He expects returns on His investments, for His efforts to pay off, as referenced in Isaiah 55:11, "11 So shall my word be ... it shall not return unto me void, but it shall accomplish that which I please, and it shall prosper in the thing whereto I sent it."

Jesus did not come to die and rise again, only for people to stay the way they were before. The Messiah came to elicit change; deep, inward, thorough change, not unlike how a caterpillar changes into a butterfly.

The change is so dramatic that the latter form is totally distinguished from its lowly past self. A law of change was commanded by Jehovah at creation, so that it would be established at the time of Jesus' resurrection. Some may view this as God requiring work for one's salvation, but on the contrary, God sees it as a natural chain of events which He expects to occur. He doesn't demand growth, He anticipates and expects it. It should happen, because there are laws in place to cause it to happen, just as when a garden is planted, then a crop is produced. A farmer would get upset if his crop didn't grow, no matter how much he watered and fertilized it. If nothing happens, it's because something went wrong, not because the farmer is being demanding.

The works of faith spoken of in James 2 are an outward showing of God's work within the individual. As Jesus says, "first clean the inside of the cup and dish, and then the outside also will be clean" (Matthew 23:26). When Paul speaks of the fruits of the spirit in Galatians 5:22-23, he is referencing the same things as James. Spiritual growth will inevitably cause a physical manifestation in a person's life.

God, as a Monarch, has created laws and guidelines to govern different parts of creation to work the way He desires. He created a set of spiritual laws, just as there are physical laws. These laws are hard and fast decrees which are written down in God's books. They do not just happen to exist; they were chosen very carefully by God before Genesis 1:1. In a way, the Lord had each person's spiritual walk in mind when He framed the laws of the universe back in the beginning. God thought ahead and therefore has an expectation. God however, does not micromanage. He has allowed people the ability to tend to their own hearts and spiritual livelihoods. Therefore, free will enters into the equation and is why we are each responsible for our own thoughts, feelings, and actions. God has given us our own hearts to steward, not unlike how He delegated authority to Adam for stewarding the earth in Genesis 2.

Although people on Earth do not always understand the laws at play in the universe, and there are certainly times of despair (just ask Job), the Lord has asked us to trust Him. Trust Him, because He knows more about what is going on than we do. God is at the top of it all. He doesn't expect each saint to be at the same spiritual development of Abraham or the Apostles. However, He does hope that each one will strive to grow. God meets all individuals where they are, and with that, comes His desire for each person to grow taller and stronger, being sanctified toward spiritual maturity.

The love of God is perfect. Just like a parent, God loves His children without condition. However, when a child is born (as wonderful as that is), parents rightly anticipate the stages of normal growth. If a child stays a child, in body or mind, for the rest of their life, a serious problem is evident. That isn't normal; it is a cause for concern. Slothful adolescents are often the worry of their parents. The parents then push and encourage the adolescents to pick themselves up and grow into adulthood. It is not because the parents do not love their children that they have expectations of growth and development: it is the opposite! If the parents love the child, they may go to extreme lengths to get their son or daughter through whatever obstacles are in their lives. God is the same way.

Looking at the Exodus story, God chose to reveal Himself as Jehovah to a nation in a way unseen before or since. The whole hope, according to the author of the book of Hebrews, was to get Israel to enter into faith (Hebrews 3). Their unbelief stopped them. God is looking inside us to see how we are growing, how we are faring. If we are receptive to His directions, there are often calmer seas. Although, it can be easy to fall off track and forget the Lord at the dock, He may still walk out to us, but this time we are caught in a storm, from which only He can rescue us. Sometimes a storm is God's plan to work in us and sometimes it's our own tomfoolery that got us into the mess to begin with. Proverbs 3:6 says, "6 In all thy ways acknowledge him, and he shall direct thy paths."

CHAPTER 7

How Long is the Bible Meant to Last?

While it was stated earlier, it bears repeating: the Bible is the complete, accurate, inspired Word of God. It is a book dictated by God to various scribes and other figures over the course of approximately 4,000 years. The divine inspiration of God's Word requires that it must have divine preservation. If this is not true, then how can one know that the Apostles read accurate renditions of Moses when they wrote their epistles? Or that Jesus in the synagogue was even able to read out of Isaiah accurately? Abraham was about as far from Jesus' birth, as Jesus' birth is from modern day.

Many people have doubted the Bible's historical authenticity. It is not a new problem. Even Israel, back in Old Testament times, did not take God's Word seriously enough. If they had, they would not have worshiped false deities time and again. However, archaeology has always come out in support of the Biblical text. A discovery in 1947 dispelled a whole swath of textual criticism: the Dead Sea Scrolls. Winton Thomas, in his book titled *Antiquity,* speaks on the Dead Sea Scrolls, listing the main discoveries:

"The discovery of [scrolls] in the cave now known as Cave I, led to the exploration of further caves in the neighborhood, and now even eleven caves in all have yielded up manuscripts. Every book of the Hebrew Old Testament except the book of Esther is represented.... The largest single deposit of manuscripts, which may turn out to be the most important of all, was found in Cave IV in 1952. From this cave tens of thousands of fragments, representing more than 380 manuscripts, have been recovered."

The discovery of these scrolls and fragments have presented an opportunity to examine the true authenticity of the Bible. Furthermore it opens a door to discuss the preservation of the Word of God. In the book *A General Introduction to the Bible*, the authors had this to say about a passage from the intact Great Isaiah scroll:

"Of the 166 words in Isaiah 53, there are only 17 letters in question. Ten of these letters are simply a matter of spelling, which does not affect the sense. Four more letters are minor stylistic changes, such as conjunctions. The three remaining letters comprise the word LIGHT, which is added in verse 11 and which does not affect the meaning greatly. Furthermore, this word is supported by the Septuagint (LXX). Thus, in one chapter of 166 words, there is only one word (three letters) in question after a thousand years of transmission — and this word does not significantly change the meaning of the passage."

While this point is hotly contested by Biblical critics, it should be mentioned that the thousand years noted above only dates to the Masoretic text, on which the KJV is based. As the KJV still remains in active use, the heritage of the Dead Sea Scrolls is brought into modern day. For further perspective, one would not be wrong in stating the differences found within the Biblical text are minimal, over the course of more than two thousand years. In a young earth model, that covers the last third of Earth's history. While changes are present, the main core, spirit, and intent of the text is clearly and without question, preserved.

As amazing as this discovery is, it does bring up a question on the preservation of the Bible. Why then, are there any differences at all? While it is plain to see that God preserved His book across history, why is it not one hundred percent the same? What is seen is rather 98-99% accuracy in the Dead Sea Scroll manuscripts. Why would God allow only this marginal level of "error?" To answer this question, one can argue that there is more error and side with the textual critics. However, that would put the power of God, and thus the entirety of the Biblical text, into question. One could argue that doing so would be simply foolish and arrogant. Again, either the Bible is the Word of God, or it isn't. Can one play around with that effectively as a half-truth?

Thus, it seems prudent to view the preservation of the Bible in the context of its appointed medium. Namely, the Scriptures were designed to exist within creation. While there is no doubt a spiritual copy sitting on God's desk that He may reference, the copies available to modern man are physical. Due to the nature of the creation in which humanity lives, everything is temporal. There are laws in place which ensure that no physical thing will last forever, but spiritual things can. Even heaven is temporal, yet it is designed to be a habitation for spiritual beings (Revelation 21:1). The physical aspects of the universe have limitations, because of their temporal nature. The temporal nature of the universe is not entirely the same as manifestations from the law of sin and death, as Peter states in I Peter 1:19-20, that Jesus' death, burial, and resurrection were planned before the foundation of the world. God, therefore, purposely chose for the *cosmos* to end up with all of the natural and spiritual laws currently in place. These are the same laws which govern the preservation of Scripture.

When the limitations of the medium within the physical realm are coupled with the archaeological proof found in the caves near Qumran, a broader perspective is uncovered. In order to grasp this broader perspective, it requires going back to God's creation. To understand how the Scriptures can be preserved, it is important to have an understanding of how God intends things to be copied. In this area, He has provided a handy comparison for textual copying found in nature. That comparison is DNA.

DNA is copied within the nucleus of each cell inside the human body. "About 330 billion cells are replaced daily, equivalent to about one percent of all our cells. In 80 to 100 days, 30 trillion will have replenished—the equivalent of a new you" (Fischetti, 2024). Each time a cell is replaced, the DNA must be copied. If the body didn't do a very good job, then people would not live very long, or they might start growing strange appendages. From time to time, this may occur due to long term radiation exposure, but that is considered abnormal.

All that said, it is well known that cancer exists. While cancer has many causes, one of those causes is genetic mutation. Such mutations can manifest within the body due to errors in coding. That is not to say that every genetic difference leads to cancer. Safe guards exist within the body which work against it (American Cancer Society, 2022). Cancers have a way of working against our immune systems: "In principle, tumor development can be controlled by cytotoxic innate and adaptive immune cells; however, as the tumor develops from neoplastic tissue to clinically detectable tumors, cancer cells evolve different mechanisms that mimic peripheral immune tolerance in order to avoid tumoricidal attack" (Gonzalez, 2018). Plainly spoken, cancer tumors have a way of getting the body to accept them as normal, when in fact they are harmful. This concept is important to remember regarding the body of Christ and how false doctrines and teachers may "creep in unawares." Christians must be on the lookout for wolves in sheep's clothing. If the wolf gets accepted into the body, it will start to form a "tumor." An excellent example of this is the many types of Scripturally divergent teachings and cults in existence which contort Christian ideals.

Peering into how God designed DNA to be copied, it can be deduced that He likely anticipated the Bible to have a similar system of quality control as that of the body. Indeed, when a scribe copied the Scriptural text, there were meticulous controls in place when doing so. However, if something was incorrect in the scribe's work, there were "external controls" also in place. For example, when someone reads a Bible verse from the pulpit, people familiar with the Words will be able to pick out whether or not there is an error. The Jewish people were very knowledgeable of the Scriptures and would frequently check and double check that the copied scrolls were correct.

In the same manner the body uses a quality control process with antibodies, the saints are meant to know the Scriptures enough to find false teachings. This ensures that any errors in the words are discovered quickly and dealt with. One of the problems with so many different English Bible translations is most people do not closely examine the words they read and the meanings behind them. Instead, discrepancies are often shrugged off. During a long enough period, there will be issues in doctrine and theology which start to show up among different denominations and sects. The Holy Spirit is very active in this quality control process. However, only if people are in tune and listening to the Spirit of God will they be able to reap the benefits of His instruction. It may be though, He says something one may not wish to hear.

The quality controls of Scriptural copying are in place so as to preserve the Word of God. While obvious, there are laws in the physical realm which naturally lead to destruction of objects. Nothing physical is meant to last forever; thus, it is necessary to copy things. When things are copied there is a need for quality control, because those same laws, working to destroy things, also work to create disorder and error. It may well be a cause of the law of sin and death, but it is hard to prove at this time. Nevertheless, God chose the physical medium to preserve the physical Bible. God knew before hand, when He gave the inspirations of the Words to the original hearers, that these issues would need to be overcome.

In this medium, much like DNA, the Scriptures had to be meticulously copied so that future generations could (and do) profit from the texts. The preservation of the Scriptures is a pure Word preserved through an impure world. Thus, it seems logical that God created a degree of "flex" in the quality controls. This flex is only on the part of "scribal errors" which do exist in a relatively minute way and are visible when comparing modern texts to the Dead Sea Scrolls. However, the

Spirit of God is still pure. And the Holy Spirit has always been present with the saints to guide them. Therefore, it can be deduced that God, aware of the problems of the medium, chose to account for this in Scriptural preservation. Any "margin of error" seen is very much like the tolerances used in machine work or the like. When things are constructed or machined, there is always a tolerance equated for in the process. An "acceptable margin of error" is where one piece can vary from another within thousandths of an inch, demonstrated in the tight standards common to aerospace manufacturing. Yet, within these standards, is still a tiny amount of variance.

The question posed at the beginning of the chapter ventures deeper into the intent and purpose of the Bible, and how God directs its preservation through an imperfect world. Again, returning to DNA, God has already shown His methods for preserving written texts (or codes) in the natural world. He expects a high level of accuracy. However, even DNA has tolerances. Every now and then a letter or two of the DNA sequence is misspelled. Ninety-nine and a half percent of the time these differences are inconsequential. The cell is able to figure out the differences and account for them. This again, is the level of "error" seen between the Dead Sea Scrolls and the Masoretic text: marginal and largely inconsequential.

One could argue with this evidence that God doesn't preserve His Word; with the originals being the only true inspired renditions. However, the archaeological facts lay plain the accuracy of God's Word over at least 2,000 years of trial and turmoil. In a similar vein, some suggest that there are books missing from the Bible, such as the books of Enoch and Jasher. Still others contend that the Masoretic text is inferior to the Septuagint for one reason or another. The vast majority of these paradigms stem from a belief that man has been able to tamper with God's Holy Word and that God has not bothered to correct these tamperings. Indeed, there is ample evidence to show that man has <u>actively</u> doctored the Words of Holy Writ for his own means. In Les Garrett's book *Which Bible Can We Trust?*, he outlines the efforts by a duo (Westcott and Hort) to alter the KJV into a revised standard of the Bible. This meddling has led to the creation of many similar English Bible translations present in the modern day.

What seems important to remember here is God's infinite power. In Job chapter 1, Satan comes before God and asks God to test Job, "12 And the Lord said unto Satan, Behold, all that he hath is in thy power; only upon himself put not forth thine hand. So Satan went forth from the presence of the Lord." A very important theological lesson is apparent: God said Satan could go so far, but no further. Satan has a leash (i.e. boundaries); he can only go as far as God allows him. In this way, God uses Satan as a tool. In fact, had it not been for Satan entering into Judas Iscariot, Jesus would not have been betrayed and turned over to the Gentiles. Only in this way was Jesus crucified and raised again from the dead, in fulfillment of Old Testament prophecy. God is smarter than Satan and his followers. God also understands them better than they do themselves and certainly better than they understand God. God in His infinite power, uses His enemies to do His will.

In the Scriptures, God even uses cleverness and cunning. In I Kings 22, God sent a lying spirit into the midst of Ahab's Baal prophets. Yet, at the same time, God sent His prophet Micaiah to warn Ahab that his false prophets were listening to a lying spirit. Foolishly, Ahab listens to the Baal prophets anyway and dies; just as the LORD had decreed. The LORD used cunning, coupled with forthright wisdom, honesty, and warning, knowing the direction Ahab would take. There is no reason to assume that God doesn't deal similarly with Satan, or even with disobedient saints. God is in control, not the devil, and certainly not mankind.

In light of these things, one could say the Scriptures are faulty, as "one error means the whole thing needs to get thrown out, because you never know what else might be wrong." This logic is foolish. Firstly, the level of error present within the Scriptures is important to keep in mind. Secondly, many people may not realize it, but every house, bridge, car, airplane, gas line, cell phone, computer, chair, and hospital life support system all have margins of error. Does that mean they are unreliable and need to be thrown out? To be considered unusable? Requiring continuous scrutiny? Showered with unwarranted criticism? Clearly not. Yet, it seems the Bible does not get the same level of treatment as other mundane objects in people's lives.

Artists understand the limits of the mediums they work with. God understands the limits of the medium He created. God is all powerful, yet there is another characteristic of God visible in how He preserves His Word. God has a willingness for us to work with Him. He has a desire for us to participate in what He is doing. As the Apostle Paul states, "Most gladly therefore will I rather glory in my infirmities, that the power of Christ may rest upon me" (I Corinthians 12:9b).

When God says He will do something, He expects us to believe it. Contrary to many belief systems, the Scriptures actually state that God preserves His Word, "6 The words of the Lord are pure words: as silver tried in a furnace of earth, purified seven times. 7 Thou shalt keep them, O Lord, thou shalt preserve them from this generation for ever" (Psalm 12:6-7). While there is disagreement on the meaning of "them" in verse seven, the layout of the text suggests that God is referring to His Words being preserved from generation to generation. Matching with the rest of Scripture, there is a connection to Psalm 119:89, "89 For ever, O Lord, thy word is settled in heaven." Jesus goes further in Matthew and says, "35 Heaven and earth shall pass away, but my words shall not pass away" (Matthew 24:35).

God tolerated the tampering of the Scriptures by Westcott and Hort for a reason. Yet, even with that allowed, God has not permitted the KJV (or other received texts) to disappear. Rather, both have been present in tandem for the last century or so. Such a duality is very striking. Why would God allow it? What can be learned about Him from this situation? Perhaps an answer lies in what the different Bible translations say and any differences in doctrine. Further discussion is best left to others for full examination.

This universe is like a plate. Be it paper or ceramic (depending on beliefs regarding the future), one thing is for sure: it is unclean. It is temporary. Useful for a time, the universe completes its purpose well, but when God is ready to clean the table off, He throws the paper plates away and cleans up the dirty ceramic ones. The Bible, in its physical form, is only meant to last until Jesus comes to reign on the earth. After that however, it would be reasonable for God to renew our copy with the one He has up top. That being said, it's probably very similar to our current reading. While the Bible is not a one time use paper plate, or even a dirty ceramic one, it's physical form is temporary. That's why it needs to be copied and that's why it needs to be carefully preserved.

BIBLIOGRAPHY

American Cancer Society (2022). Genetic Mutations | Types of Mutations. American Cancer Society. www.cancer.org/cancer/understanding-cancer/genes-and-cancer/gene-changes.html.

Bassett, DB. (2011). The Scriptural Universe. The Scriptural Universe Model. www.creationevidence.org/biblical/scriptural_universe_model.php.

Fein, Yaakov Y., et al. (2019 September, 23). Quantum Superposition of Molecules beyond 25 KDA. Nature News. Nature Publishing Group. www.nature.com/articles/s41567-019-0663-9.

Fischetti, Mark, and Christiansen, Jen. MF & JC. (2024 February, 20). Our Bodies Replace Billions of Cells Every Day." Scientific American, www.scientificamerican.com/article/our-bodies-replace-billions-of-cells-every- day/.

Geisler, Norman & Nix, William, NG & WN. A General Introduction to the Bible, Moody Press, Page 263

Gonzalez, Hugo et al. (2018). Roles of the immune system in cancer: from tumor initiation to metastatic progression. Genes & development vol. 32,19-20: 1267-1284. doi:10.1101/gad.314617.118

Irion, Robert, RI. (2011 December, 1). Opening Strange Portals in Physics. Smithsonian.Com, Smithsonian Institution, www.smithsonianmag.com/science-nature/opening-strange-portals-in-physics-92901090/.

Newton, Sir Isaac, IN. (1704). Opticks: A Treatise of the Reflexions, Refractions, Inflexions and Colours of Light."

Schroeder, Gerald (1999). Genesis One: A Physician Looks at Creation. Berg Productions.

Townsend, Paul K. PT (2022 July, 4). Aether, dark energy and string compactifications. Philosophical Transactions of the Royal Society A: Mathematical, Physical and Engineering Sciences, vol. 380, no. 2230,

Veneziano, Gabriele, GV. (2013 October, 4). The Myth of the Beginning of Time. Scientific American, www.scientificamerican.com/article/the-myth-of-the-beginning-of-time-2006-02/.

Winton, Thomas D. TDW. (1959). The Dead Sea Scrolls. Antiquity 33.131: 189–194.

Wollack, Dr. Edward J. EJW. (2016 May, 9). WMAP Big Bang CMB Test. Tests of Big Bang: The CMB, NASA, map.gsfc.nasa.gov/universe/bb_tests_cmb.html.

I grew up in the mountains and meadows of Eastern Oregon, enjoying all the beauty of God's creation. While portions of my life have been spent elsewhere, the basaltic outcroppings and aromatic sage bushes have always felt like home. Life in Eastern Oregon is more simple compared to many other places, but I believe that is one of its strongest assets. It allows one to think and reflect.

I have traveled and seen different cities and regions in the Western United States and I see how similar, yet at the same time how unique, each individual is. A very important thing often neglected in the world these days is people being still and watching others. Not just at the mall or grocery store, but in personal life as well. Too often we make assumptions without actually getting to know the people we believe are our closest, or even our farthest.

God knows us better than we know ourselves, but that's because He pays attention to us. He asks in return that we pay attention to Him. If we can truly have an interactive and personal relationship with the creator of the universe, I think that's something worth pursuing.

In fact, I have a passionate desire to deeply understand the God of the universe. The Living God, the Holy God. The God of the Bible: the Lord Jesus Christ. There are many questions surrounding Him and not all can be answered. However it is better to try, knowing the end is unachievable, than to sit having never dared enter the sea, thus forgoing all its riches. Even a shallow pearl is worth the dive.

I hope my musings contained here are able to prompt the reader into thought and discussion, and perhaps even encourage them to search for themselves other treasures God has to offer.